THE · WORLD · AROUND
SPACE

Ian Ridpath and James Muirden

Illustrated by
Ron Jobson

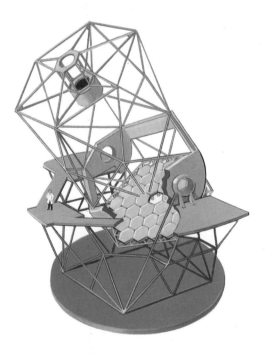

Kingfisher Books

NEW YORK

KINGFISHER BOOKS
Grisewood & Dempsey Inc.
95 Madison Avenue
New York, New York 10016

First American Paperback Edition 1992
First published in the United States
in hardcover by Warwick Press in 1991.

10 9 8 7 6 5 4 3 2 1

Copyright © Grisewood & Dempsey Ltd. 1991

Library of Congress Catalog Card Number: 92–053096
CIP Data applied for

ISBN 1–85697–814–1

Series design: The Pinpoint Design Company
Cover design: Terry Woodley
Cover illustration: Alex Pang
Printed in Spain

Contents

The Earth in Space

Our home, the Earth, is one of nine planets that orbit the star we call the Sun. The Earth is the third planet out from the Sun, at a distance of approximately 93 million miles (150 million km) from it. The Sun and its family of planets, along with various smaller pieces of orbiting debris, make up the Solar System.

The Nine Planets

The four planets closest to the Sun — Mercury, Venus, Earth, and Mars — are all small, rocky bodies. Beyond them lie four planets made mostly of gas — Jupiter, Saturn, Uranus, and Neptune. And farther away still is Pluto, a small, frozen world journeying around the edge of the Solar System.

Planets and Stars

A planet is a body that does not give out light of its own. Stars, on the other hand, glow of their own accord. The planets of our Solar System shine by reflecting light from the Sun. By contrast, stars can be seen over vast distances because they are glowing balls of gas, generating heat and light by nuclear reactions at their centers.

The Sun appears much bigger and brighter than the stars we see at night simply because it is much closer than they are. The nearest star to the Sun, Alpha Centauri, is over 25 million million miles (40 million million km) away.

Light-Years

Distances between stars are so great that they are not measured in miles, but in light-years. This is the distance a beam of light (which moves at 186,000 miles per second) travels in a year. A light-year is about 5.88 trillion miles (9.46 trillion km), which means that Alpha Centauri is 4.3 light-years away.

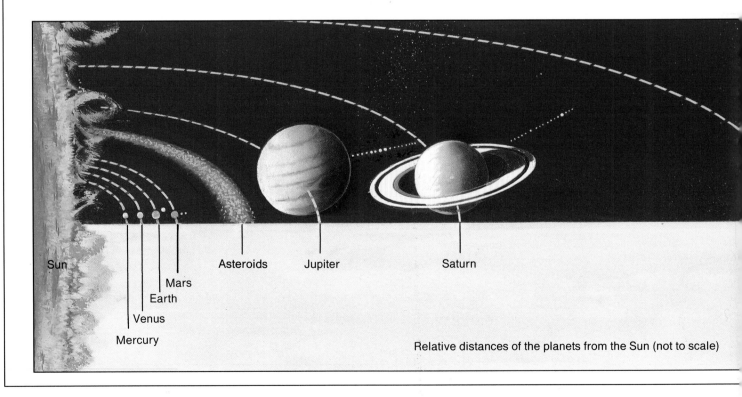

Sun Mercury Venus Earth Mars Asteroids Jupiter Saturn

Relative distances of the planets from the Sun (not to scale)

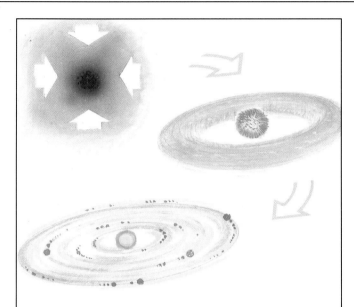

According to current ideas, the planets were born about 4.6 billion years ago from a cloud of gas and dust orbiting the Sun. Slowly, over millions of years, the specks of dust in the cloud collided and stuck together, building up into large lumps of material. Gravity pulled these larger lumps of rock and metal together, forming planets. Some debris from the original cloud still exists in the form of comets, asteroids, and meteoroids.

▲ The Earth is 7,926 miles (12,756 km) in diameter. Three-fourths of its surface is covered with water, and it is surrounded by an atmosphere of gas. From space, the Earth appears blue and white — the blue being water and the white being clouds.

The Earth spins on its axis once every 24 hours, a period we call one day. At the same time it is orbiting the Sun. One orbit around the Sun takes about 365.25 days to complete, and is called a year.

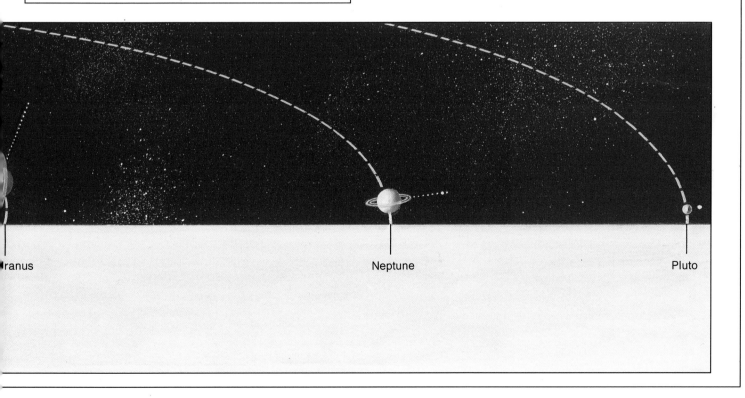

ranus   Neptune   Pluto

The Moon

The Moon is the Earth's nearest neighbor in space. It is a rocky body without air or water, 2,160 miles (3,476 km) in diameter — about one quarter the size of the Earth. The Moon lies 237,370 miles (382,000 km) from us, which is very close on the scale of the Solar System.

The Moon's Orbit

The Moon orbits the Earth about once a month — in fact, the word "month" comes from the name "moon." Early calendars were based on the motion of the Moon around the Earth, but in our modern calendar the lengths of the months have been altered somewhat, with the result that they no longer exactly match the Moon's orbital movement.

The Far Side of the Moon

As the Moon orbits the Earth it keeps one face permanently turned toward us. Until quite recently, no one had seen the Moon's far side. Now, space probes have shown that it is covered with craters and rugged mountains, and is even rougher than the near side.

▶ Because the Moon is close to us it was a natural target for astronauts. In the American Apollo program, six teams of astronauts landed on the Moon to collect rocks and explore its surface. The first landing, by Neil Armstrong and Edwin Aldrin, was made in July 1969, and the last in December 1972.

From the rock samples the astronauts brought back, geologists have found that the dark lowland plains of the Moon are at least 3 billion years old, and the brightest highlands are older still. Evidently, the Moon was heavily bombarded from space much earlier in its history, when most of the craters were formed, but for the past 3 billion years it seems to have remained relatively unchanged.

▶ When the Moon is close to the Sun in the sky, all the brightly lit portion is turned away from us and the Moon is invisible (New Moon). As the Moon moves around the Earth we at first see a thin crescent, and then a half-illuminated Moon (First Quarter). When the Moon is opposite the Sun in the sky we see it fully illuminated (Full Moon).

As the Moon moves from New to Full it is said to be waxing. As it moves back to New Moon again it is said to be waning.

▼ The surface of the Moon is pockmarked with craters of all sizes, up to 120 miles (193 km) or more in diameter. There are also dark lowland plains, which make up the familiar Man-in-the-Moon we see from Earth.

Most astronomers agree that the largest craters were caused by impacts from meteorites, but there may also be some small volcanoes on the Moon. Volcanic lava apparently once flooded out into the low-lying regions of the Moon, forming the dark-colored lunar plains.

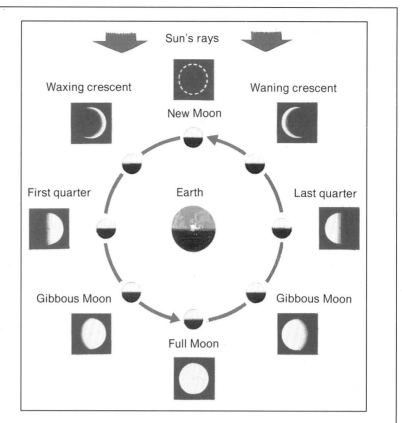

Mercury

Mercury, the closest known planet to the Sun, is a small rocky body 3,030 miles (4,876 km) in diameter — only one and a half times the size of our own Moon. It orbits the Sun every 88 days at an average distance of 36 million miles (58 million km), and rotates on its axis very slowly, once every 59 days.

The Scorched Planet

Space probes have shown Mercury to be scarred by numerous craters caused by bombardment from meteorites, while its lowland plains appear to have been flooded by volcanic lava. Conditions on the planet are extreme. It has no air or water, and on the side facing the Sun, the surface temperature rises to 780°F (416°C), hot enough to melt tin and lead. On the side turned away from the Sun, the temperature falls to a chilling 275°F (170°C) below zero.

Bathed in dangerous radiation from the Sun, Mercury must be far too hostile for any form of life and would certainly be very unhealthy for astronauts to visit.

Venus

Venus is the second planet from the Sun, at a distance of 67 million miles (108 million km). It is surrounded by thick clouds which totally obscure its surface. These clouds reflect the Sun's light strongly, making Venus the most brilliant planet visible from Earth.

Danger Beneath the Clouds

Venus is similar in size to the Earth, but the similarity ends there. The planet's atmosphere consists mainly of unbreathable carbon dioxide gas. This traps heat from the Sun like a blanket, forcing temperatures to a furnacelike 850°F (455°C). The atmosphere bears down with a pressure 90 times greater than that of the Earth. The famous clouds are not made of water vapor, like those on Earth, but consist of concentrated sulfuric acid. Anyone who went there would be crushed, roasted, suffocated, and melted by the acid, all at the same time!

▲ Several space probes have reached Venus and sent back close-up pictures of its dense acid clouds.

▼ Soviet Venera probes have reached the surface of Venus and sent back information and pictures. The probes were soon destroyed by the lethal conditions on the planet's surface.

Mars

Mars, the first planet beyond the Earth, has fascinated people for centuries because of the possibility that it might support life. Mars is about half the size of Earth, with a diameter of 4,220 miles (6,790 km). It orbits the Sun every 687 days at a distance of around 142 million miles (228 million km). It is the most similar planet to Earth, with a day only a little longer than ours.

Signs of Life?

The American astronomer Percival Lowell thought that he saw canals on Mars, perhaps used by Martians to bring water from the ice caps at the poles to their crops at the equator. But other astronomers could not see the canals, and probes have shown that they do not exist.

The red color of Mars is caused by large areas of desert, and by dust in the atmosphere.

Mars has two small, lumpy moons called Phobos and Deimos. They are about 14 miles (22 km) and 7 miles (11 km) across respectively, and are probably former asteroids which were long ago captured by the pull of the planet's gravity.

▲ The Viking space probe landers photographed the red, desertlike surface of Mars while miniature on-board laboratories tested the dusty Martian soil for any signs of life.

THE MARTIAN LANDSCAPE

Space probes have found that Mars is a dead and desolate world covered with scars and craters. Some of the craters were probably formed by the impact of meteorites crashing in from Space. Others are actually volcanoes.

The largest volcano, called *Olympus Mons* (Mount Olympus), is 300 miles (480 km) wide and 12 miles (19 km) high, making it the largest known volcano in the Solar System.

The planet also has a vast network of valleys called the *Valles Marineris* (Mariner Valley), which extend over thousands of miles. Some of these valleys are 3 miles (5 km) deep — the Grand Canyon in Arizona would be lost inside them!

Mars has turned out to be less welcoming than previously thought. Its atmosphere, made of carbon dioxide, is as thin as the air 20 miles (32 km) above the Earth. There is no rainfall, and even on a summer afternoon, temperatures at the surface of Mars do not rise above freezing point.

Photographs taken by the various probes orbiting Mars showed no sign of life on the planet, not even patches of vegetation. But that did not rule out the possibility of small plants such as cacti on the surface, or creatures living in the soil. The only way to find out was to land and look . . .

▲ Olympus Mons   ▼ Martian Rift Valley

LANDING ON MARS

In 1976, two American Viking space probes landed on Mars to look for life. Their cameras showed the surface to be a red-colored desert covered with loose boulders and stones. The sky is pink, caused by particles of dust in the atmosphere.

The probes carried on board an automatic biology laboratory, which tested samples of Martian soil to see if any tiny bugs or bacteria were living in it. No definite signs of anything living or growing were found. It is possible that some form of life exists on parts of the planet not visited by the Viking landers, but it does not seem very likely. Most astronomers now believe that there is no life on Mars. One day, astronauts will visit the red planet and perhaps set up permanent bases there.

Jupiter

At a distance of 483 million miles (778 million km), Jupiter is considerably farther away from the Sun than its neighbor Mars. It is a gigantic planet, containing 2.5 times as much matter as all the other planets put together. Its diameter of 88,700 miles (142,750 km) is about 11 times that of the Earth.

Nearly a Star

Despite its size, Jupiter is made mostly of the lightest matter in the Universe, the gases hydrogen and helium. This means that Jupiter is very similar in composition to the Sun, and if the planet had been at least ten times bigger and heavier, it would have begun to glow like a small star. As it is, Jupiter gives off twice as much heat as it receives from the Sun.

Beneath Jupiter's Clouds

When you look at Jupiter through a telescope you see a swirling mass of multicolored clouds around the planet. These are drawn out into bands by its rapid rotation of just under ten hours — the fastest "day" of any planet in the Solar System. The colors in the clouds, mostly red, brown, and yellow, are caused by various chemicals in the atmosphere.

Jupiter has no solid surface at all. Instead, the gases of which the planet is made become more and more tightly packed together until they are compressed into liquid. At its center, Jupiter is mostly liquid hydrogen and helium, although within this there may be a small core of rocky material.

▼Giant Jupiter has a large family of moons.

JUPITER'S GREAT RED SPOT

There is only one permanent feature in the ever-changing clouds of Jupiter. It is an oval shape aptly named the Great Red Spot, big enough to swallow three Earths laid side by side. It is usually red in color but can also appear pink or brown.

The Red Spot was first seen through telescopes in 1666. To begin with, some astronomers thought it might be the vent of a fiery volcano, but that theory was soon dismissed. Later theories suggested it could be an object floating in the clouds.

Pictures from the two Voyager space probes in 1979 cleared up the mystery by showing the Red Spot to be nothing more than a spinning whirlpool of cloud. Other whirling colored spots appear in the clouds of Jupiter from time to time, but none is as big as the Great Red Spot and none lasts so long.

JUPITER'S MANY MOONS

Jupiter has a family of at least 16 moons. The four largest — Ganymede, Io, Callisto, and Europa — were first seen by the Italian scientist Galileo Galilei in 1610. They are all visible from Earth through a simple pair of binoculars. Two of these so-called Galilean moons, Ganymede and Callisto, are larger than the planet Mercury.

In 1979 the Voyager space probes discovered impact craters and ice patches on Ganymede and Callisto. Most startlingly, volcanoes were spotted erupting on another moon, Io, whose surface is covered with orange and yellow deposits of salt and sulfur. The Voyager probes also found that Jupiter is encircled by a thin ring of rocky debris, too faint to be seen from Earth.

Saturn

Saturn, the sixth planet in line from the Sun, is the most distant planet visible with the naked eye. At 74,600 miles (120,000 km) in diameter, it is second only in size to its neighbor Jupiter. Like Jupiter, it also spins very fast — a day lasts 10.14 hours. Saturn takes 29.5 years to orbit the Sun at a distance of 888,200,000 miles (1,430 million km).

The Most Beautiful Planet

Saturn is widely regarded as the most beautiful planet in the Solar System, because of the bright rings that surround it. These rings are not solid, as they may at first appear, but consist of countless tiny moonlets orbiting the planet.

Apart from its rings, Saturn is a scaled-down version of Jupiter. The two planets are made of much the same materials — mostly hydrogen and helium gas.

Light Enough to Float

Saturn is unique in one respect. The gases of which it is made are not as densely compressed as the gases of Jupiter and, in fact, Saturn has an overall density less than that of water. Therefore, given a big enough ocean, the giant planet would float!

Masses of Moons

Saturn has at least 24 moons, the largest of which is Titan, with a diameter of 3,000 miles (4,830 km). Titan is the only satellite known to have a substantial atmosphere. This contains chemicals that can support life, although no one expects to find living organisms at a temperature of −290°F (−179°C).

SATURN'S RINGS

Saturn's rings were discovered by the Dutch astronomer Christian Huygens in 1659. For years it was thought that Saturn was unique in this respect, but more recently it has been discovered that Jupiter, Uranus, and Neptune all have ring systems as well.

It took astronomers many years to find out exactly what Saturn's rings are made of. We now know that they consist of chunks of rock about the size of bricks, orbiting the planet. These probably represent the building blocks of a moon that never formed. The particles of rock are coated with ice, which makes them appear very bright.

Saturn's rings extend for 150,000 miles (241,000 km) from rim to rim, yet their thickness from top to bottom is only about 6 miles (10 km). Seen edge on, therefore, they are almost invisible. In relation to their diameter, the rings of Saturn are thinner than a sheet taken from a newspaper.

The outermost part of the rings is called Ring A. It is separated from the brightest and widest part of the rings, Ring B, by a 1,700-mile (2,700-km) gap called Cassini's Division, named after the French astronomer who detected it in 1675. The thin Ring C, also known as the Crepe Ring, lies inside Ring B. The Voyager spacecraft showed that these rings contain hundreds of separate ringlets.

Uranus

Uranus was discovered in 1781 by William Herschel. It is a gas ball 32,000 miles (51,500 km) in diameter, and appears greenish due to the large amounts of methane in its atmosphere.

Uranus orbits the Sun every 84 years, at a distance of 1.78 billion miles (2.87 billion km). The planet's axis is tilted, as though it has been in a massive collision. As a result, each polar region has about 40 years of sunlight followed by the same period of darkness.

In 1977, astronomers discovered that Uranus is encircled by faint rings of rocky debris. In 1986, *Voyager 2* found 13 narrow rings and traces of others, as well as ten new moons in addition to the five already known.

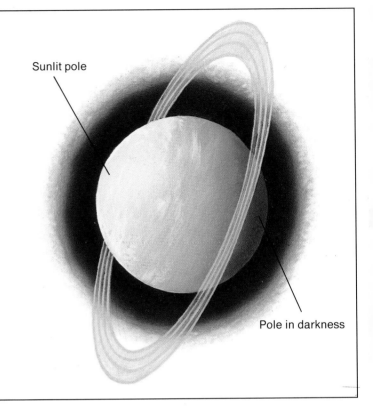

Sunlit pole

Pole in darkness

Neptune

Some 60 years after the discovery of Uranus, astronomers found a planet even farther out in the Solar System — Neptune. This turned out to be a near twin of Uranus.

Neptune's cloudy, bluish atmosphere, photographed by *Voyager 2* in 1989, contains some definite markings, including the Great Dark Spot, a spinning storm cloud as large as the Earth.

Neptune appears to rotate in about 18 hours 20 minutes, although hurricane-force winds in the atmosphere drive some clouds around more quickly. It has a faint and narrow ring system, as well as eight moons. Neptune is 2.8 billion miles (4.5 billion km) away from the Sun and takes 165 years to complete one orbit.

Pluto

At the outer edge of the Solar System lies an almost unknown world. Pluto is so small and faint that it was not discovered until 1930, in a photographic search for new planets.

Not a True Planet?

With a diameter of just 1,370 miles (2,205 km), Pluto is the smallest planet in the Solar System. Some astronomers think it too small to be called a proper planet, and that it could be either an escaped moon or satellite of Neptune, or the largest of a distant belt of asteroids.

Charon, Pluto's tiny satellite, was not discovered until 1978. These two tiny worlds orbit each other in six days nine hours, with the same hemispheres always facing each other, and take 248 years to orbit the Sun.

An Eccentric Orbit

Although Pluto is on average the farthest planet from the Sun, its orbit is the most eccentric or irregular in the Solar System, and for a short time in each of its "years" it is closer to the Sun than Neptune. This is the case at present. From 1979 to 1999, Neptune, not Pluto, is the outermost planet of the Solar System.

Debris in Space

In addition to the major planets, the Solar System contains thousands of minor planets, known as asteroids. Most asteroids orbit the Sun in a belt between Mars and Jupiter, but there are some which stray across the paths of the planets. If one of these wandering asteroids hit the Earth, it would cause devastation on a massive scale.

Asteroids

Asteroids are rubble left over from the formation of the Solar System. They are made of rock and metal, like the Earth and other inner planets. There are thousands of asteroids, of all shapes and sizes. The largest, Ceres, is 620 miles (1,000 km) in diameter and orbits the Sun every 4.6 years. It was the first asteroid to be discovered, in 1801.

Meteorites

Occasionally, lumps of rock or metal known as meteorites crash to Earth from space. These are probably fragments which are broken off asteroids by collisions.

If a meteorite is traveling fast enough when it strikes the ground, it can make an enormous crater. This is what happened in the Arizona desert when a meteorite plunged 570 feet (175 m) into the ground. This crater is three-fourths of a mile (1.2 km) in diameter. It is believed to have been formed about 20,000 years ago by the impact of an iron meteorite that may have weighed as much as a quarter of a million tons. Most of the meteorite was destroyed in the blast, but several tons of iron fragments scattered over a wide area.

Fortunately, most meteorites are traveling

The Arizona meteorite crater

too slowly when they hit the ground to cause much damage, although some have smashed roofs and windows.

The Largest Meteorite
The largest known meteorite lies where it fell in prehistoric times, near Grootfontein in Namibia. It weighs over 60 tons.

Shooting Stars
On any clear night, you can see several meteors, or shooting stars, flash across the heavens. These are particles of dust, probably from comets, which burn up when they enter the Earth's upper atmosphere.

A typical meteor is about the size of a grain of sand. Its dying blaze of glory lasts for less than a second.

COMETS
Comets are ghostly wanderers in the Solar System. They consist of loose rock and dust welded together by frozen gas. Astronomers think they may come from a cloud of billions of comets far beyond Pluto.

Comets travel on long, looping orbits between the planets, spending much of their time in the dark and cold outer reaches of the Solar System where they are invisible.

When a comet approaches the Sun it begins to warm up and glow. Gas and dust stream away from its head to form a twin flowing tail which can be millions of miles long. The dust in one tail reflects the sunlight and appears yellow. The gas tail on the other hand appears blue.

About 1,000 comets are known, some of which can be easily seen with the naked eye. The most famous is Halley's comet, sightings of which can be traced far back into history. William the Conqueror is known to have seen it in 1066.

Halley's comet returns to the vicinity of the Sun every 76 years. It last appeared in 1986, when close-up photographs of it were taken by the European Space Agency's probe *Giotto*.

The Sun

The Sun is our parent star. Without its heat and light there would be no life on Earth. It is a flaming ball of gas 865,000 miles (1,392,000 km) in diameter. A line of 109 Earths could fit across the Sun, and it contains as much material as a third of a million Earths.

Incredible Temperatures

The Sun is made almost entirely of hydrogen and helium gas. Its surface has a temperature of 10,000°F (5,500°C), but at its center temperatures rise to an unimaginable 25 million degrees.

The Sun's surface is frequently dotted with spots and eruptions. Explosions over sunspots, known as flares, throw off particles which travel through space and can cause radio interference on Earth. From time to time, giant looping arches of gas, known as prominences, are seen extending from the Sun's surface.

The Sun's visible surface is called the photosphere. Around this is a faint halo of thin gas called the corona, which is normally invisible. The corona can nevertheless be seen with special instruments, or when the Moon blocks off the body of the Sun from our view during a total eclipse.

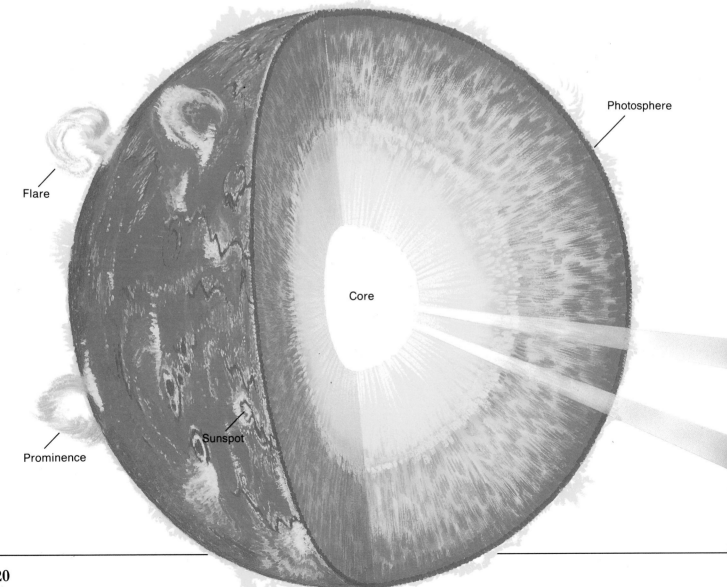

Flare

Prominence

Sunspot

Core

Photosphere

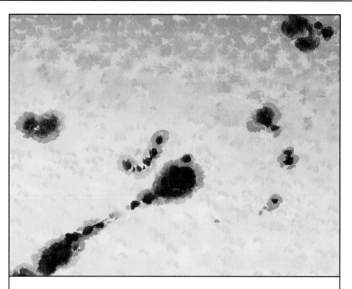

ECLIPSES

When the Moon passes between the Earth and the Sun, it blots out the Sun's light to produce an eclipse. If only part of the Sun is hidden by the Moon, we see a partial eclipse. When all of the Sun's brilliant disk is blocked out, we see a total eclipse.

During total eclipses, which can last five minutes or more, the sky becomes dark and the faint outer halo of the Sun becomes visible.

The Moon can also be eclipsed. This happens when it passes into the shadow of the Earth, and out of the Sun's light. It usually happens about twice a year somewhere on Earth.

SUNSPOTS

Dark patches known as sunspots are frequently seen on the face of the Sun. These are areas of cooler gas which do not glow as brightly as the surrounding photosphere. Most sunspots are larger than the Earth and some form groups that stretch for 100,000 miles (160,000 km) or more — half the distance from the Earth to the Moon.

The number of visible sunspots varies in a cycle of about 11 years. For several days no spots may appear at all, but at times of maximum activity, ten or more sunspot groups may be visible at a time. Some scientists believe that sunspot activity affects weather on Earth.

▼In fusion, four hydrogen atoms (H) are converted into one atom of helium (He). In the process, heat and light are produced.

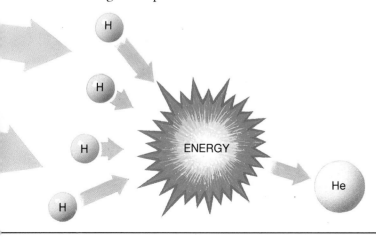

◄The Sun does not burn like an ordinary fire. Instead, its center is like a gigantic nuclear reactor. Here, constant nuclear reactions called fusion are taking place. This violent process is what happens in a hydrogen bomb.

Through fusion, the Sun is slowly changing itself from hydrogen into helium. Each second, 600 million tons of hydrogen in the Sun fuse together to become helium, with 4 million tons of hydrogen being converted into energy in the process.

Even at this rate of energy generation, the Sun can live for 10 billion years. It is currently about halfway through that life span.

The Life of a Star

Stars are born from giant clouds of gas and dust known as nebulae. Some of these, including the famous Orion Nebula shown on the next page, can be seen from Earth as fuzzy glowing patches in the night sky.

How Stars are Formed

A nebula can give rise to several stars. Star formation begins when parts of the cloud start to contract, or pull together, under the force of their own gravity, forming blobs of gas. Each blob continues to contract until the temperature and pressure at its center become so extreme that nuclear reactions begin. The blob then begins to glow, giving out its own light and heat. A new star has been born.

Red Giants

A star creates energy at its center by the steady fusion of hydrogen into helium in nuclear reactions. After billions of years have passed, it

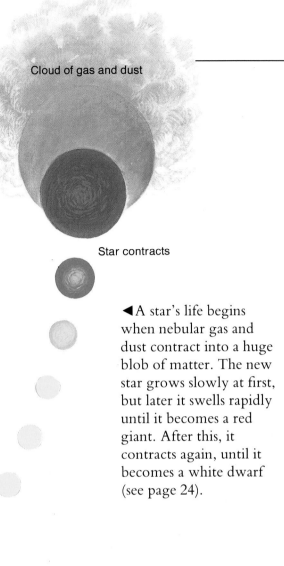

Cloud of gas and dust

Star contracts

◄A star's life begins when nebular gas and dust contract into a huge blob of matter. The new star grows slowly at first, but later it swells rapidly until it becomes a red giant. After this, it contracts again, until it becomes a white dwarf (see page 24).

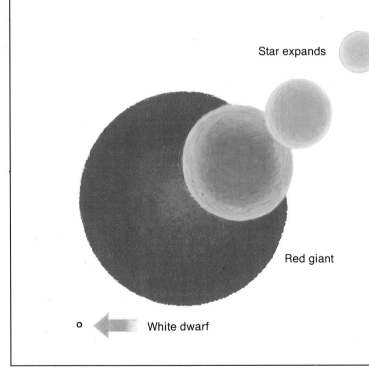

Star expands

Red giant

White dwarf

starts to use up its hydrogen fuel more quickly. When this happens, the star becomes bigger and brighter, swelling into what is known as a red giant. Red giants are immense red stars, far bigger and brighter than our Sun.

When the Sun itself becomes a red giant, it will swell to such a size that it will certainly swallow Mercury, Venus, and possibly even the Earth.

Fortunately, the Sun is currently in a stable condition. It is not expected to turn into a red giant for about 5 billion years, so we are quite safe at present!

◄The Orion Nebula is 1,500 light years away from Earth, and 40 light years across. The hydrogen gas within the nebula shines because radiation from nearby stars makes it give out energy in the form of light.

The nebula lies near the three stars that form the "belt" of the constellation known as Orion. A constellation is a group of stars which seem from Earth to be near each other, even though they may really be huge distances apart.

▼The Pleiades, or Seven Sisters, are the most famous star cluster in the sky. They lie in the constellation of Taurus. About half a dozen members of the Pleiades are visible to the naked eye, but telescopes reveal that the cluster contains a total of about 200 stars. The brightest stars in Pleiades are young blue giants, far hotter and brighter than our Sun.

The stars of the Pleiades may be only a few million years old. Our Sun was probably a member of a similar cluster when it came into being, around 4.6 billion years ago.

Star Death

Once a star becomes a red giant, it is nearing the end of its life. The thin outer gas layers of the red giant slowly drift off into space, forming a beautiful smoke ring effect. Many such stellar smoke rings, like the colorful Ring Nebula in the constellation Lyra (below), are visible through telescopes. They are called planetary nebulae because they resemble the rounded disk of a planet.

White Dwarfs

At the center of a planetary nebula is the core of the former red giant, a tiny, hot star known as a white dwarf.

A white dwarf is likely to be about 100 times smaller than the Sun — that is, about the size of the Earth. The matter in a white dwarf is densely compressed and a single spoonful of it would weigh 10 tons.

Over billions of years, the white dwarf cools off, eventually fading away into invisibility. How long a star lives depends on how much material it contains. Stars that are smaller and cooler than the Sun live the longest, whereas bigger, hotter stars burn out more quickly.

Supernovas

The stars which contain the most matter — with at least four or five times as much as the Sun — die in spectacular fashion. After such a star becomes a red giant, it erupts in a nuclear holocaust known as a supernova. For a few weeks or months the star's brightness increases billions of times as it throws off its outer layers

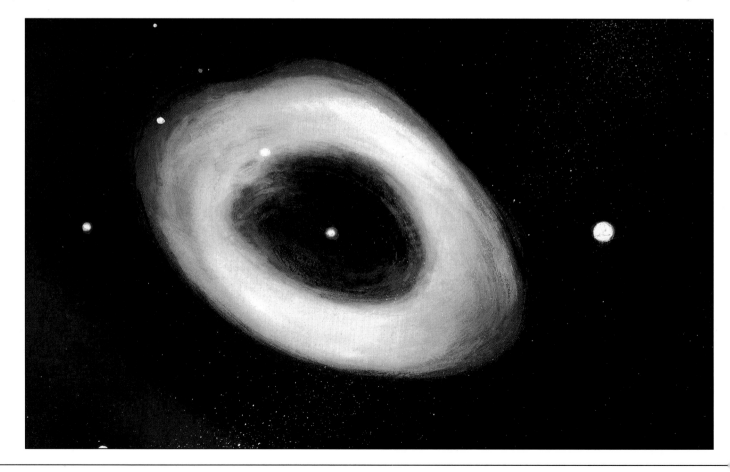

into space. The famous Crab Nebula (right) is the shattered remains of a star that astronomers saw erupt as a supernova in the year 1054.

Neutron Stars

A star does not always destroy itself entirely in a supernova. Sometimes its core is left behind, compressed into an object even smaller and denser than a white dwarf. Such a tiny super-dense object is called a neutron star and is 1,000 times smaller than a white dwarf. A spoonful of it would weigh a billion tons. Neutron stars are invisible from Earth, but some, called pulsars, can be detected from the pulses of radio waves they emit as they spin. The fastest is spinning at an incredible 622 times a second!

▲ The Crab Nebula is a huge cloud of expanding gas. It is the result of a star explosion that was seen almost 1,000 years ago from Earth. At the center of the nebula is a neutron star, spinning at a rate of 30 times per second.

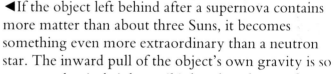

◄ If the object left behind after a supernova contains more matter than about three Suns, it becomes something even more extraordinary than a neutron star. The inward pull of the object's own gravity is so great that it shrinks until it has shrunk out of sight, becoming what is known as a black hole. Nothing can escape from the gravity of a black hole, not even the star's own light, so that it is completely invisible. However, things can fall into one. Black holes are like a bottomless drain in the universe, dragging in anything which comes within reach.

Special Stars

Not all stars are as well behaved in their light output as the Sun. Some change in brightness over periods of days, weeks, or even years. They are known as variable stars. Red giants are among the most common stars of this type.

Cepheid Variables

Some variable stars change in brightness regularly, every few days. This regularity is due to their continually swelling and contracting. These stars are named Cepheid variables.

The brightness of a Cepheid variable is related to the length of its cycle of light changes. The longer the cycle, the brighter the star. Astronomers can therefore calculate the brightness by measuring the star's period of variation. They can compare this with the actual brightness of the star as seen from Earth since this varies depending on how far away the star is. From these calculations they can work out the distance from Earth of the Cepheid variable and other stars around it.

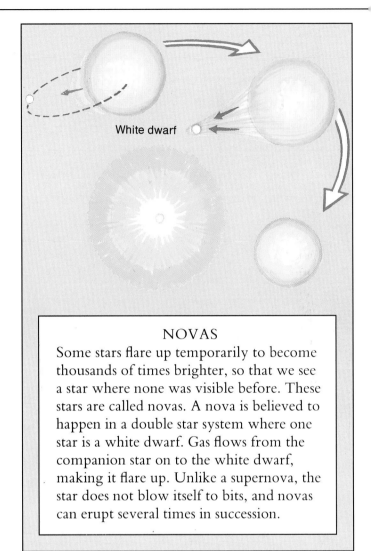

White dwarf

NOVAS

Some stars flare up temporarily to become thousands of times brighter, so that we see a star where none was visible before. These stars are called novas. A nova is believed to happen in a double star system where one star is a white dwarf. Gas flows from the companion star on to the white dwarf, making it flare up. Unlike a supernova, the star does not blow itself to bits, and novas can erupt several times in succession.

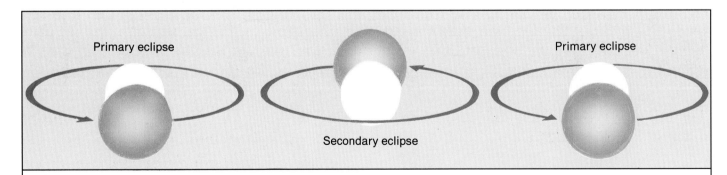

Primary eclipse

Secondary eclipse

Primary eclipse

ECLIPSING BINARIES

In some double star systems, one star periodically moves in front of the other as seen from Earth, thereby eclipsing it. When this happens, the total light we see from the system drops temporarily.

Such stars are known as eclipsing binaries. They come under the heading of variable stars, even though the stars themselves do not really change in brightness at all.

A famous eclipsing binary star is Algol, in the constellation Perseus. It consists of a faint yellow star and a bright blue one. Algol's light drops noticeably every 69 hours as the fainter star eclipses the brighter one.

This makes Cepheid variables important distance indicators in Space.

Double and Multiple Stars

Unlike the Sun, most stars exist in groups of two, three, or even more. These are known as double and multiple stars.

In some double star systems, the stars are so close that they are distorted by each other's gravity, and hot gas flows from one to another or even spirals off into space.

The stars of a double or multiple system differ greatly in size, brightness, and color. For instance, the star Zeta Aurigae consists of a red giant orbited by a small blue star. The picture above shows the spectacular view that might be had from a planet in Zeta Aurigae's solar system.

Galaxies

Our Sun is just one of more than 100,000 million stars that together make up the vast star system known as the Galaxy. If we could view our galaxy from far out in space, we would see it as a spiral of stars, 100,000 light years across and 2,000 light years thick.

The Milky Way

All the stars we see in the night sky are relatively close to us in the Galaxy — mostly within about 1,000 light years. The more distant stars of the Galaxy form a faint band of light that we can see crossing the sky on dark nights. This band, which is the thickest part of our galaxy, is called the Milky Way.

Telescopes show the Milky Way to be made up of millions of faint stars seemingly crowded upon each other. Confusingly, the name Milky Way is often also used as an alternative title for the whole of the Galaxy.

More than one Galaxy

Astronomers used to think that our galaxy and the stars within it were all that existed in the entire universe. Then, in the 1920s, the American astronomer Edwin Hubble found there were other galaxies far beyond our own in outer space.

The first object Hubble identified as another galaxy was a fuzzy patch which is just visible to the naked eye in the constellation Andromeda. Using the large 100-inch reflecting telescope on Mount Wilson in California, Hubble found that this fuzzy patch was actually made up of huge numbers of faint stars far off in space.

The object Hubble saw is now known as the Andromeda galaxy. It lies at a distance of 2.2 million light years from us, which means that we are seeing it now it as it appeared 2.2 million years ago. It is the most distant object visible to the naked eye.

A plan and side view of the Milky Way, a huge pinwheel of stars, dust, and gas. The Sun (arrowed) is situated 30,000 light years from the center, in one of the Galaxy's star-studded spiral arms. Astronomers can never see the Galaxy as it is shown here, but they can calculate its size and shape by comparing their observations with those of other galaxies.

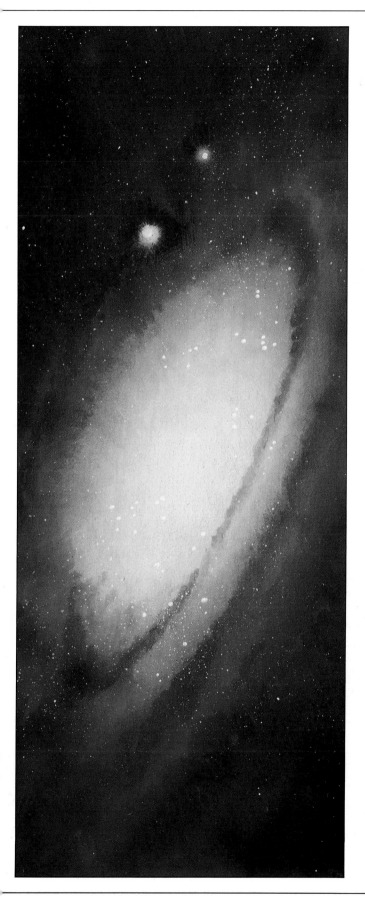

▲ A spiral galaxy

▲ A barred spiral galaxy

▲ An elliptical galaxy

◄The Andromeda galaxy is one of millions that have now been identified. Most galaxies come in one of three basic shapes, the most common being spiral, such as Andromeda and the Milky Way. About one quarter of galaxies are barred spirals — similar to spirals, but with a bar of stars across their centers. The third type, elliptical galaxies, are less common. They are like flattened balls, with no spiral arms.

The Origin of the Universe

How did the universe begin? We may never know for sure, but different scientists have come up with three main theories.

The Big Bang

After the 1920s, when Edwin Hubble first discovered that the universe was expanding, the Belgian astronomer Georges Lemaître suggested that the universe had begun in a massive explosion called the Big Bang.

According to Lemaître, all the matter in the universe was once compressed in one spot, and was sent flying outward by the Big Bang explosion. The Big Bang therefore marks the origin of the universe as we know it, although the cause of the explosion, and what happened before it, is a mystery.

If the outward movements of the galaxies are traced backward, astronomers are able to calculate when they were all crammed together. Modern measurements suggest that the Big Bang occurred between 10 billion and 20 billion years ago.

Big Bang

The Steady State Theory

A second theory of the universe was put forward in 1948. The so-called Steady State theory states that the universe never had a specific beginning. New matter is conjured into being out of empty space all the time, and the universe expands to make room. According to this theory, the universe will always look much the same.

Evidence Against the Theory

Few astronomers now support the Steady State theory, as it seems that the universe did appear very different in the past. Flaring objects known as quasars have been found far off in space, and since their light has taken billions of years to reach us, we see them as they were early in the history of the universe. Quasars are thought to be galaxies in the process of formation. There are no quasars around today, so they must have all become galaxies as the universe has grown older.

THE OSCILLATING UNIVERSE THEORY

This third theory is a modification of the Big Bang idea. It says that the universe continually expands and contracts in cycles, and the present expansion will eventually slow down and stop, to be replaced by contraction to another Big Bang, setting the process off again.

However, there is no sign that the expansion of the universe will ever stop. According to current evidence, the universe will continue to expand for ever, gradually thinning out until all the stars have died and eternal darkness descends.

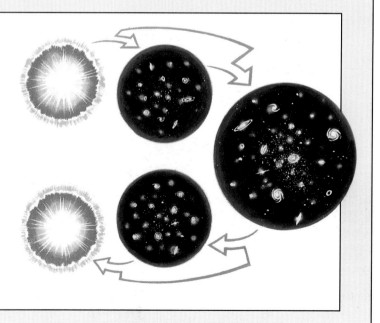

Studying Space

Astronomers study space through telescopes. A telescope collects more light than the human eye, allowing us to see objects much fainter than would otherwise be visible. The largest telescopes show stars and galaxies ten million times fainter than those visible to the naked eye. Telescopes can also magnify objects, making them seem much closer to us.

Different Types of Telescope

There are two main types of telescope — refractors and reflectors. A refracting telescope collects light with a lens. Reflecting telescopes use a main mirror instead of a lens.

No one knows who invented the telescope, but the credit is usually given to the Dutch optician Hans Lippershey, who assembled a refractor in 1608 using spectacle lenses. Soon afterward, the Italian scientist Galileo built a simple telescope of his own. With it he discovered the craters of the Moon, the satellites of Jupiter, and the phases of Venus.

The first reflecting telescope was built by the English scientist Isaac Newton in 1668.

Today's Giant Telescopes

Both types of telescope are still widely used, but the largest telescopes are all reflectors. The world's largest refractor, at the Yerkes

▼The eyepiece of a reflecting telescope can be either at the side of the tube or in a hole in the center of the main mirror.

◀A refractor uses a main lens at the front to collect light and focus it. The image can be seen in detail through another lens, called the eyepiece.

▼In a reflector, light is collected by a concave (dish-shaped) main mirror, and reflected into an eyepiece.

Observatory in Wisconsin, has a main lens 40 inches (100 cm) in diameter. The largest single-mirror reflector, in Russia, is 20 feet (6 m) in diameter.

These days, astronomers do not often look through telescopes. Instead they take pictures of objects, either as photographs or, more recently, as electronic recordings.

▼ Objects in space give out radio waves which can be picked up by radio telescopes. These collect radio waves in a large dish, in the same way as a TV satellite dish. The biggest single radio dish in the world, shown here, is in the mountains at Arecibo, Puerto Rico. It is 1,000 feet (305 m) in diameter.

► The Keck reflector in Hawaii is a new design of reflecting telescope. Instead of having just one mirror, it uses 36 separate mirrors joined together to form a huge reflective surface 33 feet (10 m) across. This collects four times more light than the 200-inch (5-m) reflector at Mount Palomar, California.

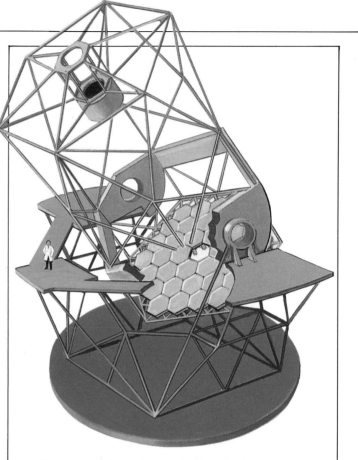

Hexagonal mirrors form a single reflecting surface.

33

Rockets

A Saturn V rocket

Rockets were probably invented by the Chinese over 750 years ago. Their rockets were like fireworks, with gunpowder as the fuel. Most modern rockets use liquid fuels but they work in essentially the same way as a firework. Inside the rocket, fuel is burned to produce hot gas. The force of the gas escaping at high speed is what pushes the rocket along.

The usual fuels for modern rockets are kerosene or liquid hydrogen. Fuel cannot burn without oxygen and there is no oxygen in airless space. So a rocket carries its own supply of oxygen, also in liquid form.

Bigger and Bigger Rockets

An American called Robert H. Goddard built the world's first liquid-fueled rocket in 1926, but it did not fly very far. A much bigger rocket, called the V2, was designed by Wernher von Braun for the German army to use during World War II.

After the war, von Braun and his colleagues moved to the United States where they continued working on rockets for space research. They designed the world's largest rocket, the Saturn V, which took men to the Moon.

DEFYING EARTH'S GRAVITY

Everything in the universe exerts a pull on everything else around it. This pull is called gravity. Because it is so large, the Earth has a very strong gravitational pull. This is what keeps our feet on the ground, the water in the oceans, and the air in the sky.

To travel from Earth into space, an object must travel with enough force to overcome the pull of gravity. To do this it must go very quickly indeed.

Imagine throwing a ball into the air (**1**). It rises a little before falling back. If you throw the ball faster (**2**), it goes higher before falling back again. If it could be thrown at a speed of 5 miles (8 km) per second (**3**), it would go into orbit around the Earth, becoming an artificial satellite. Artificial satellites orbit at heights of about 100 miles (160 km) or more.

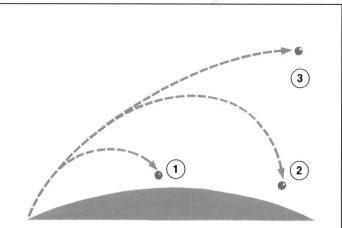

Large rockets can reach the speed necessary to put an object into orbit around the Earth. To escape Earth's gravity completely and move off into space, the rocket must go faster still — at about 7 miles (11 km) per second, or about 25,000 miles per hour (40,000 km/h). This speed is called escape velocity.

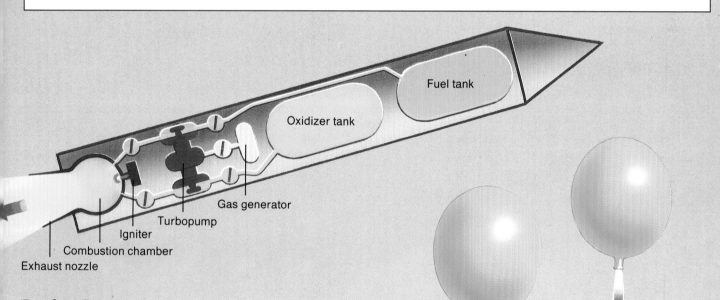

Fuel tank

Oxidizer tank

Gas generator

Turbopump

Igniter

Combustion chamber

Exhaust nozzle

Rocket Stages

Rockets are built in several stages. Each stage is a separate rocket, the bottom one being the most powerful. This stage begins to burn at launch and takes the rocket into the air.

When each stage runs out of fuel, it falls away and the next stage takes over. Therefore the rocket gets lighter as it climbs higher, and it can go faster than if it were carrying unwanted empty fuel tanks.

▲In a liquid-propellant rocket, the fuel and the liquid oxygen are stored in separate tanks. The liquid oxygen is converted into gas and pumped into the combustion chamber. There it mixes with the liquid fuel and is ignited. The resulting explosion thrusts the rocket forward with enormous force. This is the same principle that makes a balloon shoot forward when the air inside it is allowed to escape.

The Saturn V rocket burned up over 2,000 tons of fuel in the first 50 miles (80 km) of flight!

Artificial Satellites

▲ The first satellite to be put into orbit was *Sputnik 1*. It was launched by the Soviet Union on October 4, 1957. This date marked the start of the Space Age.

   Sputnik 1 was a sphere 23 inches (58 cm) in diameter with long radio antennas. It circled the Earth in 96 minutes, sending out radio signals so that scientists could track it around its orbit. It reentered the Earth's atmosphere after three months and was burned up.

▼ Some satellites are designed to photograph clouds and to measure temperatures in the atmosphere. This helps meteorologists monitor weather conditions and make better forecasts. The first such weather satellite, *Tiros 1*, was launched in 1960.

A man-made object orbiting the Earth is known as an artificial satellite. Since the first satellite was launched in 1957, the area of space around the Earth has become increasingly cluttered with them — over 2,000 have been launched to date. Not all of these are still in orbit though, because satellites are gradually slowed down by the thin gases of the outer atmosphere until they fall back toward Earth. They are then burned up, but sometimes pieces of a satellite survive and crash on Earth like artificial meteorites.

   Satellites are used for many purposes, from scientific research to military spying. They form a vital part of modern communications systems, relaying messages and television pictures right around the world.

The first living creature to orbit the Earth was a female dog called Laika. She traveled in a special compartment in *Sputnik 2*, which was launched in November 1957. Laika died in space as there was no way to bring her back.

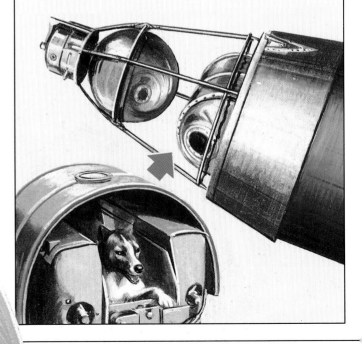

◄Satellites can detect radiation that does not get through the Earth's atmosphere, such as infrared and X rays. IRAS is used to observe infrared rays from cool objects in the Solar System and from young, invisible stars.

▼The Hubble Space Telescope operates beyond the Earth's atmosphere and is designed to take space observation into a new age. Unfortunately, a flaw in its main mirror is reducing its effectiveness.

THE HUBBLE SPACE TELESCOPE
(1) Light rays
(2) Door
(3) Primary mirror
(4) Instruments
(5) Solar panels
(6) Communication antennas
(7) Secondary mirror

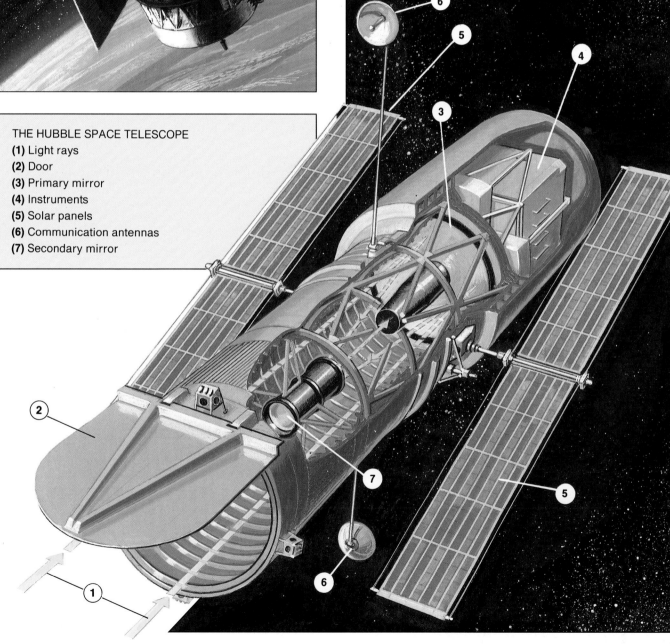

Space Probes

Space probes are unmanned exploration craft. They send back valuable information to scientists on Earth.

The Early Probes

In 1959, the Soviet *Luna 3* probe gave us the first ever view of the side of the Moon that never faces the Earth. Later Soviet probes used a remote-controlled craft called the Lunokhod to explore the Moon's surface.

In the meantime, probes sent up by the U.S. helped prepare the way for the later manned landings. The Lunar Orbiter series mapped out the whole of the Moon, while the Surveyor craft made exploratory landings.

Planetary Probes

Probes have now reached all of the planets except Pluto, and have made landings on Mercury, Venus, and Mars. *Voyager 2*, launched in 1977, inspected Jupiter and Saturn, Uranus, Neptune, and their satellites during its 12-year journey.

More recent space probes are extending our knowledge of the Solar System. They include the Jupiter probe *Galileo*, launched in 1989, and *Magellan*, which went into orbit around Venus in 1990. That year also saw the launch of the ambitious *Ulysses* probe, designed to fly over the Sun's poles and transmit valuable new information on our star.

Surveyor 3

Luna 3

Lunokhod

The *Galileo* probe shown below was launched from the space shuttle *Atlantis*. It passed Venus, using the planet's gravity to fling it in a new path toward Jupiter.

Galileo fires off a probe into Jupiter's atmosphere.

Travel in Space

On April 12, 1961, the Soviet cosmonaut Yuri Gagarin became the first human in Space, orbiting the Earth once in *Vostok 1*. His flight showed that a person could survive in Space without any ill effects. Five more Soviet cosmonauts later orbited the Earth in Vostok spacecraft, including the first spacewoman, Valentina Tereshkova.

The first American astronaut, Alan Shepard, flew in a single-seat, cone-shaped capsule called *Mercury* in 1962. This was followed by a larger craft called *Gemini* which housed two crew.

PIONEERS IN SPACE

Both Vostok (above) and Mercury (above left) were tiny spacecraft, with room for just one space pilot. Vostok was 7 feet (2 m) in diameter and about 16 feet (5 m) long. Mercury was even shorter — a mere $9\frac{1}{2}$ feet (3 m)!

A modified version of the Vostok craft, called Voskohod, had room for two or even three people. It was from one of these craft that cosmonaut Alexei Leonov performed the first space walk on March 18, 1965.

The final Mercury flight was in 1963. *Gemini 1* was sent up in March 1965, and the first of several space walks from Gemini craft (left) took place later that year.

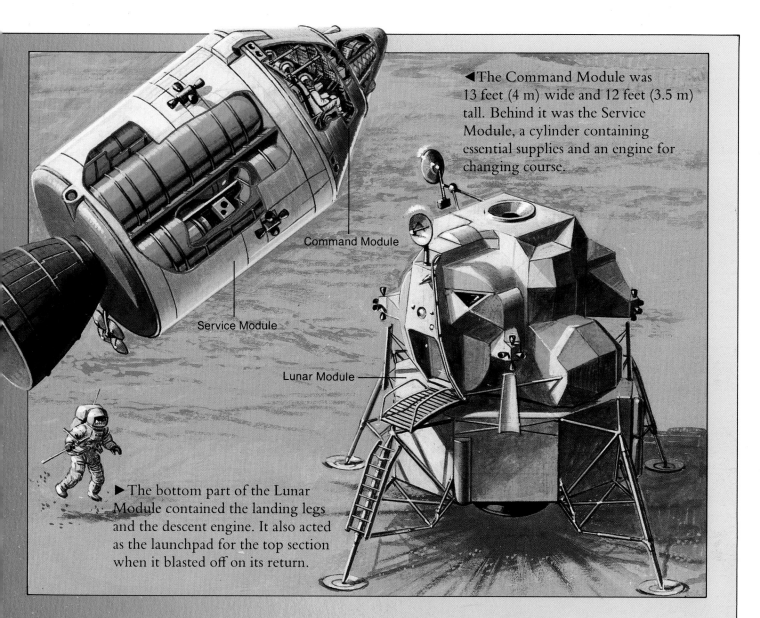

Command Module

Service Module

Lunar Module

◄The Command Module was 13 feet (4 m) wide and 12 feet (3.5 m) tall. Behind it was the Service Module, a cylinder containing essential supplies and an engine for changing course.

►The bottom part of the Lunar Module contained the landing legs and the descent engine. It also acted as the launchpad for the top section when it blasted off on its return.

The Apollo Missions

Once space travel had become a reality, the next great ambition was to reach the Moon. This was achieved by the U.S. Apollo program in 1969.

Apollo was a three-man craft, sent into space on the Saturn V rocket. The crew traveled in the Command Module which sat on top of the Service Module. Beneath these two modules was the Lunar Module, the spidery craft which would actually touch down on the Moon.

Landing on the Moon

On the way to the Moon, the Apollo astronauts turned the Command and Service Modules and docked with the Lunar Module. Two astronauts crawled into the Lunar Module and guided it down to the surface. Astronauts Neil Armstrong and Edwin Aldrin made the first Moon landing on July 20, 1969, on the *Apollo 11* mission. Altogether there were six successful Apollo missions to the Moon, and the last crew spent three days on the surface before returning home.

Space Stations

To live and work in space for long periods, astronauts need more room than normal spacecraft allow. So large space stations have been launched that are capable of housing a crew for several months.

Living in space takes a lot of getting used to. Astronauts have to take lots of exercise to keep themselves fit and to help their bodies adjust to the lack of gravity.

The First Space Stations

The U.S. Skylab space station (below), was launched into space on May 14, 1973. The craft was used over a period of about six months, until February 8, 1974.

The first Soviet space station, called Salyut 1, was launched in April 1971, and six others followed during the next 15 years. Their crews set new records for endurance in space, with missions of as much as a year.

What Next?

At present, the only manned object in Space is the latest Soviet space station, Mir ("Peace"). It was launched in 1986.

The United States has not used a space station since Skylab, but there are plans to assemble a much larger craft before the end of the century. Called Freedom, it will have living quarters for eight people. The space station will be launched in pieces by the Space Shuttle and assembled in Earth's orbit.

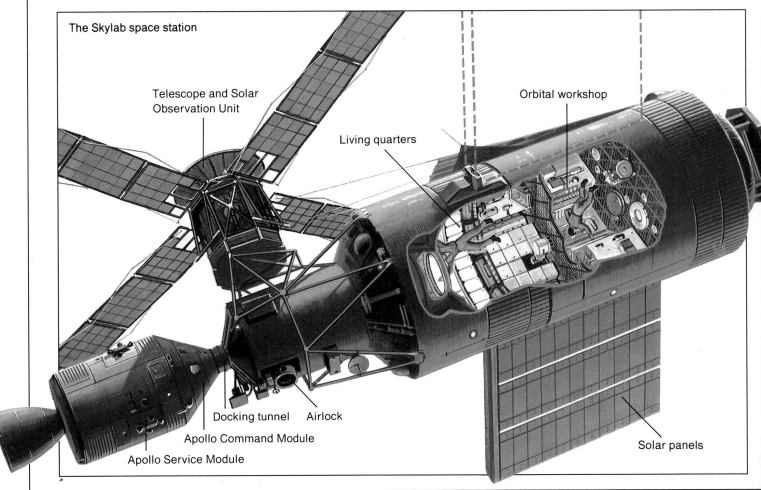

The Skylab space station

Telescope and Solar Observation Unit

Orbital workshop

Living quarters

Docking tunnel   Airlock

Apollo Command Module

Apollo Service Module

Solar panels

SKYLAB

Skylab, shown opposite, was an orbiting laboratory, carrying cameras and other equipment to survey the surface of the Earth, as well as a battery of telescopes with which to observe space. It had room for three astronauts.

Altogether, the craft was occupied for 171 days, by three different crews. The third crew stayed for three months, which was the longest period spent in space at that time.

In addition to observing the Sun, the stars, and the bright comet Kohoutek, the Skylab crews examined the effects of weightlessness and airlessness on living and non-living things.

Skylab gradually lost height, and plunged to a fiery end in the atmosphere in July 1979.

MIR

Launched on February 19, 1986, the Soviet space station Mir, seen above, has grown considerably from the initial 60-feet long craft. It has gradually been built up into a large complex, with the addition of several extra modules each weighing up to 20 tons. Spacecraft have constantly docked with the space station, bringing new equipment and provisions as well as replacement crews.

The most important of the additional modules has been the 12-ton Kvant ("quantum") observatory. It is 20 feet (6 m) long and 13 feet (4 m) across, and contains five different telescopes as well as a laboratory for space biology.

Recent events in Russia have caused the withdrawal of all crew members from Mir.

A New Era in Space

The American Space Shuttle has opened up a new era in spaceflight. Previously, all rockets and manned spacecraft were used only once. After each mission they were scrapped, which made spaceflight very expensive. The Space Shuttle on the other hand is a combined launch rocket and manned spacecraft that can be recovered and reused many times.

The Shuttle has three main engines which are fed with fuel from a massive tank on which it "rides" into orbit. Two extra rockets are attached to the sides to help boost the craft at launch. Two minutes after takeoff, the extra rockets fall away, parachuting into the ocean, where they are recovered for reuse. Powered by its main engines, the Shuttle continues into orbit. The large fuel tank has to be jettisoned and cannot be used again.

The Shuttle Missions

The Shuttle has flown dozens of missions, using four different craft. The first flight, by *Columbia*, was in 1981. In 1986, another craft, *Challenger*, exploded. After this there were no more flights for two years. The replacement for *Challenger* is *Endeavor*: the other two craft are *Discovery* and *Atlantis*.

The Shuttle is designed to stay in orbit for at least ten days, although most flights have lasted about a week. When its mission is finished, it glides back through the atmosphere. Insulating tiles protect its outer surface from the heat from reentering the atmosphere. The craft completes its mission by landing on a runway like an ordinary plane.

▼The part of the Space Shuttle which actually goes into space is a winged craft the size of a jet airliner. This can carry up to eight people as well as up to 29 tons of freight in its huge cargo bay.

One of the Shuttle's roles has been to transport satellites (including the Hubble Space Telescope) into orbit. Some of these have been communications satellites for television and telephone transmissions, the launch costs paid for by commercial businesses.

It has also rescued faulty satellites, either repairing them in space or bringing them back to Earth.

The Space Shuttle has also been used for various scientific purposes. It has carried the European Space Agency Spacelab, which enabled scientists to carry out a number of experiments away from the pull of the Earth's gravity.

The Space Shuttle with Spacelab on board

The different stages of a Space Shuttle mission: The Shuttle is launched by a rocket, orbits as a spacecraft, and lands like a glider. This has led to great reductions in the cost of spaceflight as each Shuttle can be used up to 100 times.

The Future

At the beginning of this century, few would have predicted that within 100 years people would have landed on the Moon and sent spacecraft to the edges of the Solar System. We may be certain that the 21st century will bring equally amazing leaps forward.

Journeys to the Stars?

The problem with traveling to the stars is that they are so far away. At today's speeds, spacecraft would take 100,000 years to reach even the nearest star, Alpha Centauri.

To reach the stars in a shorter time, we must develop new and faster rockets, far in advance of those that exist today. The solution seems many years away, but it may well lie in the use of nuclear power.

Space Colonies

One development that does seem possible in the next century is the construction of giant space colonies with room for thousands of people. These are likely to be spheres or cylinders, rotating to provide artificial gravity on the inside.

The colonies will probably be landscaped to look as much like the Earth as possible. They may be completely self-contained, growing their own food and using solar power as a limitless source of energy.

Useful Words

Asteroid A solid lump of matter that circles the Sun. Most asteroids are to be found between the orbits of Mars and Jupiter. They come in all shapes and sizes, up to 600 miles (960 km) across.

Atmosphere A layer of gases that surrounds some planets and moons. The Earth's atmosphere extends for about 1,000 miles (1,600 km) above the surface. It consists of a particular mixture of gases that we call air.

Big Bang An expression used to describe the massive explosion which many scientists think marked the beginning of the universe.

Black hole The result of a supernova collapsing completely under its own gravity. Black holes cannot be seen, but anything around them is sucked in, never to appear again.

Comet A small ball of frozen gas and dust that orbits around the Sun. Sometimes a comet's orbit brings it close to the Sun, while at other times it may be way out at the farthest edges of the Solar System.

Crater A hole in the ground made when the ground is struck by a solid body such as a meteorite.

Galaxy One of the countless star systems that are to be found throughout the universe. Our Galaxy, the Milky Way, contains at least 100,000 million stars, including our own Sun.

Gravity The pull that all bodies in the universe exert on each other. All the planets in the Solar System are held in their orbits by the immense pull of the Sun's gravity.

Light-year The enormous distance traveled by light in one year, equivalent to about 5.88 trillion miles (9.5 trillion km).

Meteor A bright streak in the sky caused by a particle of dust from space burning up as it enters the Earth's atmosphere.

Meteorite A lump of rock or metal that travels through the Earth's atmosphere and strikes the ground. Fortunately, few meteorites cause much damage when they land.

Moon A solid body that orbits a planet. Moons are also called satellites.

Multiple stars Two or more stars orbiting closely around each other. The Sun is unusual in being a single star, as most stars are part of multiple star systems.

Nebula A huge cloud of glowing gas and dust from which stars are formed.

Orbit The looping path through space followed by one body traveling around another body. The Moon orbits the Earth, and the Earth orbits the Sun.

Planet A sizable ball of matter that orbits a star. The only planets that we know exist are the nine in our own Solar System.

Red giant An aging star that has swollen and become much brighter than it was before.

Satellite A body that orbits a planet or star. The Earth is orbited by one natural satellite — the Moon — and by all sorts of artificial satellites sent up into orbit from the ground.

Solar System Our star, the Sun, together with everything that orbits it — the nine planets, their satellites and various bits and pieces of debris.

Star A massive ball of matter that produces heat and light through nuclear reactions taking place inside it.

Supernova The explosion that takes place when an especially massive star has become a red giant.

White dwarf A hot bright star that is smaller than our Sun. A star becomes a white dwarf after it has been through the red giant phase.

Index